# SUMMER MATH WORKBOOK

## Bridge Building Activities

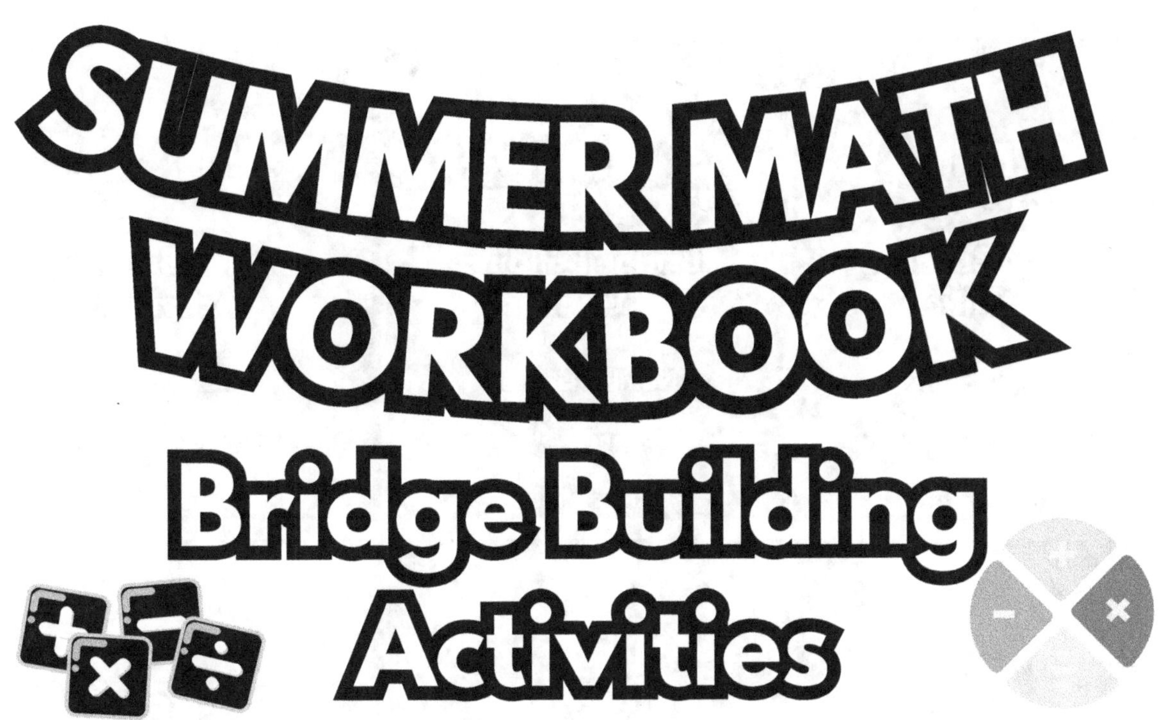

Grade
1 → 2
SUMMER MATH WORKBOOK
Bridge Building Activities
Number Sense
Addition and Subtraction
Place Value

Grade
2 → 3
SUMMER MATH WORKBOOK
Bridge Building Activities
Number Sense
Addition and Subtraction
Place Value

Grade
3 → 4
SUMMER MATH WORKBOOK
Bridge Building Activities
Number Sense
Addition and Subtraction
Place Value

Grade
4 → 5
SUMMER MATH WORKBOOK
Bridge Building Activities
Multiplication and Division
Place Value and Units
Fractions and Geometry



Grade
5 → 6
SUMMER MATH WORKBOOK
Bridge Building Activities
Multiplication and Division
Factors and Multiples
Fractions and Geometry



Grade
6 → 7
SUMMER MATH WORKBOOK
Bridge Building Activities
Arithmetic
Algebra
Geometry and Statistics

Grade
7 → 8
SUMMER MATH WORKBOOK
Bridge Building Activities
Ratio and Percentage
Algebra and Cartesian Plane
Geometry and Statistics



Grade
8 → 9
SUMMER MATH WORKBOOK
Bridge Building Activities
Ratio and Percentage
Algebra
Geometry and Graphing



Grade
9 → 10
SUMMER MATH WORKBOOK
Bridge Building Activities
Factoring and Distributing
Algebra
Geometry and Graphing

# Introduction

As parents and educators, we understand the pivotal role that mathematics plays in shaping a child's academic journey and future success. Yet, the path to mathematical proficiency can often seem daunting, filled with challenges and complexities. That's where the transformative power of Summer Bridge Building Activities books comes into play, illuminating the way forward with clarity, precision, and purpose.

Summer vacation is a time for rest and relaxation, but it also presents the risk of the "summer slide," where students lose some of the academic gains they made during the school year. Summer Bridge Building Activities books are specifically designed to tackle this challenge, ensuring that your child stays academically engaged and prepared for the upcoming school year. These books provide a seamless bridge from one grade to the next, reinforcing essential skills and introducing new concepts that will give your child a head start.

Imagine your child eagerly diving into the pages of a Summer Bridge Building Activities book, greeted by clear, engaging content that demystifies complex mathematical concepts. With each turn of the pages, they embark on a journey of discovery, encountering thoughtfully curated practice questions that reinforce learning and sharpen problem-solving skills. As they unveil the answers to those questions, a sense of accomplishment blossoms within them — a tangible reward for their hard work and dedication.

Summer Bridge Building Activities books transcend traditional educational tools; they are meticulously crafted to build a deep and enduring understanding of mathematics. These books follow a sequential and logical progression, starting from fundamental principles and advancing to sophisticated problem-solving strategies. Each chapter is designed to build on the previous one, ensuring a solid and comprehensive foundation for future learning.

Parents, we yearn for nothing more than to see our children thrive academically and personally. We want to witness the spark of inspiration ignited within them as they overcome academic challenges with confidence and poise. Summer Bridge Building Activities books serve as indispensable partners in this noble endeavor, offering not just practice questions but the keys to unlocking a world of academic and personal opportunities.

Visualize the pride on your child's face as they master a challenging math concept, the joy they experience when their efforts yield results, and the confidence they gain with each success. These pages are designed to make learning math a positive, enriching, and deeply rewarding experience that will benefit them throughout their academic journey and beyond.

For educators, Summer Bridge Building Activities books are invaluable allies in the quest to cultivate mathematical proficiency in the classroom. Accompanied by comprehensive guides and readily available answers, instructors can focus on mentoring and nurturing their students, secure in the knowledge that these books provide a robust framework for effective learning.

Within the pages of Summer Bridge Building Activities books lies not just the promise of academic excellence, but the seeds of a brighter future. By integrating these resources into your child's summer routine, you are bestowing upon them the gifts of confidence, curiosity, and a lifelong love of learning.

Invest in your child's future today with Summer Bridge Building Activities books — because every great journey begins with a single step, and this step can change everything. Keep the momentum of learning alive over the summer, and watch your child soar to new academic heights.

# Contents


| | |
|---|---|
| **Equations (One Side)** | **1** |
| **Equations (Two Sides)** | **6** |
| **Order of Operations (PEMDAS)** | **11** |
| **Solving Equations** | **17** |
| **Solving Inequalities** | **24** |
| **Simplify Expressions** | **34** |
| **Linear Equations** | **40** |
| **Find Slope from two Points** | **43** |
| **Graphing Linear Equations** | **46** |
| **System of Equations** | **51** |
| **Quadratic Equations** | **58** |

Grade
7 - 9
PRE ALGEBRA
WORKBOOK
BRIDGE BUILDING
ACTIVITIES
Equations, Inequalities and Expressions
Linear Equations Graphing and Slope
System of Equations Quadratic Equations

Grade
6 - 8
PRE ALGEBRA
WORKBOOK
BRIDGE BUILDING
ACTIVITIES
Equations One Side and Two Sides
Verbal Algebra Expressions
Linear Equations and Slope Order of Operations

Grade
5 - 6
PRE ALGEBRA
WORKBOOK
BRIDGE BUILDING
ACTIVITIES
Integers, Mixed Numbers Decimals and Fractions
Place Value Exponents and Roots
Percentage and Ratio Word Problems

PRE ALGEBRA
WORKBOOK
for
Beginners
Integers Fractions, Mixed Numbers
Place Value Exponents and Roots
Percentage Ratio Conversion

PRE ALGEBRA
WORKBOOK
for
Adults
Integers Percent and Ratio
Equations, Inequalities Expressions
Order of Operations

Grade
7 - 8
PRE ALGEBRA
WORKBOOK
BRIDGE BUILDING
ACTIVITIES
Equations, Inequalities and Expressions
Verbal Algebra Expressions
Percent and Ratio Word Problems


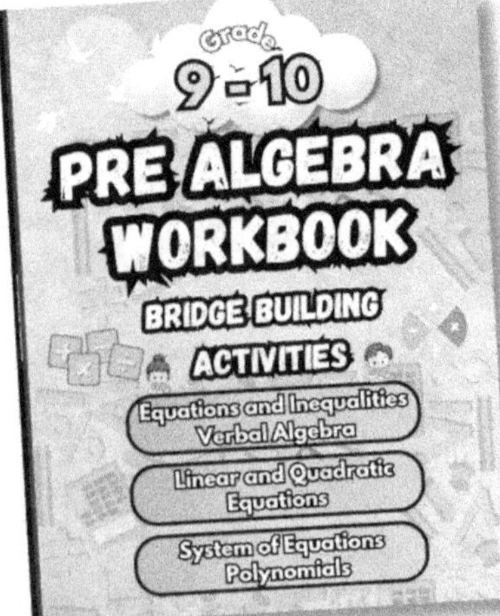

Grade
9 - 10
PRE ALGEBRA
WORKBOOK
BRIDGE BUILDING
ACTIVITIES
Equations and Inequalities Verbal Algebra
Linear and Quadratic Equations
System of Equations Polynomials

Grade
8th
ALGEBRA 1
WORKBOOK
BRIDGE BUILDING
ACTIVITIES
Order of Operations
One and Two Step Equations and Expressions
Linear Equations Cartesian Plane

Grade
7 - 9
ALGEBRA 1
WORKBOOK
BRIDGE BUILDING
ACTIVITIES
Integers Order of Operations
One and Multi Step Equations and Expressions
Linear, Quadratic Equations Equations One Side, Two Sides

<u>**Solving Equations (One Side)**</u>

Solving one-step equations involves performing a single operation to isolate the variable and find its value.

Let's solve an equation step by step: $16 + x = 31$

1. Identify the Goal:

   The goal is to isolate the variable $x$ on one side of the equation.

2. Simplify the Equation: Combine like terms on both sides of the equation, if necessary.

   The equation is already simplified.

3. Undo Addition or Subtraction: If there's addition or subtraction involving the variable, undo it by performing the opposite operation on both sides of the equation.

   Since $x$ is being added to 16, we'll undo this operation by subtracting 16 from both sides of the equation:
   $$16 + x - 16 = 31 - 16$$

4. Isolate the Variable: Ensure that the variable is alone on one side of the equation.
   $$x = 15$$

5. Check Your Solution: Substitute the value of $x$ back into the original equation to verify that it satisfies the equation.
   $$16 + 15 = 31$$
   $$31 = 31$$

The equation is balanced.

## Equations (One Side)

Solve for the variable.

**1)** $5 + y = 15$

**2)** $1z + 5 = 12$

**3)** $z - 3 = 5$

**4)** $9k + 8 = 17$

**5)** $9 - k = 1$

**6)** $12 \div k = 4$

**7)** $x \times 7 = 21$

**8)** $20 - 3z = 2$

**9)** $7 + 6y = 19$

**10)** $1k + 6 = 12$

11) $8z - 10 = 54$

12) $60 \div y = 6$

13) $4 \div m = 1$

14) $10 \div y = 1$

15) $5 + 2x = 21$

16) $72 \div z = 9$

17) $z + 2 = 5$

18) $m \div 3 = 5$

19) $4 - m = 0$

20) $2m - 3 = 3$

**21)** $10m + 6 = 56$

**22)** $5m - 6 = 39$

**23)** $32 - 5k = 7$

**24)** $21 - 2m = 3$

**25)** $m - 2 = 6$

**26)** $3m + 4 = 10$

**27)** $6m + 2 = 26$

**28)** $54 - 8k = 6$

**29)** $y \times 10 = 10$

**30)** $m - 7 = 3$

**31)** $3 \times z = 30$

**32)** $z \times 2 = 18$

**33)** $7m - 4 = 59$

**34)** $6m + 4 = 34$

**35)** $1 + 7x = 43$

**36)** $k \div 5 = 4$

**37)** $7 + 9y = 97$

**38)** $2 \div x = 2$

**39)** $2 \times z = 12$

**40)** $m \times 5 = 45$

**41)** $x + 1 = 2$

**42)** $18 - 3y = 3$

**43)** $5z - 8 = 32$

**44)** $6 + 5m = 46$

**45)** $6 \times k = 24$

**46)** $6y + 9 = 69$

**47)** $10 + 1x = 12$

**48)** $z \div 1 = 7$

**49)** $7z + 5 = 12$

**50)** $57 - 8k = 1$

<u>**Equations (Two Sides)**</u>

A two-sided equation is an equation where both sides have expressions with variables and constants. The goal when solving a two-sided equation is to find the value of the variable that makes both sides equal.

For example: Let's solve an equation:

$$9 + 8x + 8 = 64 + x + 2$$

- Combine Like Terms: Simplify each side of the equation by combining like terms (terms with the same variable or constants).

$$9 + 8x + 8 = 64 + x + 2$$
$$17 + 8x = 66 + x$$

- Isolate the Variable: Use inverse operations to isolate the variable on one side of the equation.

subtract $x$ from both sides:
$$17 + 8x - x = 66 + x - x$$
$$17 + 7x = 66$$

subtracting 17 from both sides:
$$17 - 17 + 7x = 66 - 17$$
$$7x = 49$$

divide both sides by 7:
$$\frac{7x}{7} = \frac{49}{7} = x = 7$$

- Check Solution: Once you find the solution, substitute it back into the original equation to ensure it makes the equation true.

Substitute $x = 7$ back into the original equation:
$$9 + 8(7) + 8 = 64 + 7 + 2$$
$$9 + 56 + 8 = 64 + 7 + 2$$
$$73 = 73$$

## Equations (Two Sides)

Solve for the variable.

**1)** $27 - m = 3 + 5m$

**2)** $45 + y = 6y + 5$

**3)** $4 - y = 3y$

**4)** $5y = 24 - y$

**5)** $29 + x = 4 + 6x$

**6)** $11 + z = 9 + 2z$

**7)** $4 + y = 4y + 1$

**8)** $5k = 36 - k$

**9)** $36 - k = 9 + 2k$

**10)** $18 + y = 4y$

**11)** $27 + z = 4z$

**12)** $7z = 54 + z$

**13)** $34 - z = 3z + 2$

**14)** $49 - z = 4 + 4z$

**15)** $25 + m = 1 + 7m$

**16)** $16 + z = 8 + 5z$

**17)** $8 - k = 7k$

**18)** $12 - y = 2y$

**19)** $56 - m = 6m$

**20)** $36 - k = 7k + 4$

**21)** $8 + 7z = 26 + z$

**22)** $7x = 48 - x$

**23)** $5 + 2m = 14 - m$

**24)** $34 - z = 2 + 7z$

**25)** $35 - x = 4x$

**26)** $2m + 3 = 6 + m$

**27)** $65 - m = 8m + 2$

**28)** $3 + 3x = 21 + x$

**29)** $6m = 28 - m$

**30)** $39 + y = 9 + 7y$

**31)** $63 - x = 6x$

**32)** $4x + 1 = 26 - x$

**33)** $8 + y = 1 + 2y$

**34)** $21 - x = 2x$

**35)** $13 - y = 8 + 4y$

**36)** $9 + z = 3 + 2z$

**37)** $35 + m = 6m$

**38)** $4y + 5 = 50 - y$

**39)** $13 + m = 8 + 2m$

**40)** $2k + 2 = 17 - k$

**41)** $8 + x = 2x$

**42)** $2k = 5 + k$

**43)** $6k = 5 + k$

**44)** $4 + 4y = 13 + y$

**45)** $6 + k = 7k$

**46)** $22 - m = 2m + 7$

**47)** $9 + m = 4m$

**48)** $21 - y = 7 + 6y$

<u>**Order of Operations (PEMDAS)**</u>

The order of operations, often remembered by the acronym PEMDAS, stands for:

- **Parentheses**: Perform operations inside parentheses first.
- **Exponents**: Evaluate exponents (powers and roots) next.
- **Multiplication and Division**: Perform multiplication and division from left to right.
- **Addition and Subtraction:** Perform addition and subtraction from left to right.

The order of operations helps to clarify which operations should be performed first in a mathematical expression to ensure consistent and accurate results.

- **Parentheses**: Evaluate expressions within parentheses first. If there are nested parentheses, start with the innermost ones and work your way out.

    1. Example: $2 \times ( 3 + 4) = 2 \times 7 = 14$

- **Exponents**: Evaluate expressions with exponents (powers and roots) next.

    1. Example: $2^3 + 4 = 8 + 4 = 12$

- **Multiplication and Division**: Perform multiplication and division from left to right.

    1. Example: $2 \times 3 + 4 = 6 + 4 = 10$

    2. Example: $6 \div 2 \times 3 = 3 \times 3 = 9$

- **Addition and Subtraction**: Perform addition and subtraction from left to right.

    1. Example: $2 + 3 \times 4 = 2 + 12 = 14$

    2. Example: $10 - 4 \div 2 = 10 - 2 = 8$

## Order of Operations (PEMDAS)

Evaluate Expressions.

**1)** $2 + 8 + 10 =$

**2)** $(8 + 6)(9 + 10) =$

**3)** $10 + 4^2 + 1 + 5^2 =$

**4)** $(3 + 3) \div 3 =$

**5)** $(1 + 1)^2 =$

**6)** $6 + 3 - 9 + 2 =$

**7)** $(9 + 3)^2 + (8 + 4)^2 =$

**8)** $7 \times 6 + 2 =$

**9)** $(2 + 10) \times (9 + 1) =$

**10)** $(1^2) \times (5^2) + 8 =$

**11)** $9 + 8 + 2 =$

**12)** $(1 \times 4) - (7 + 6) =$

**13)** $(6 + 8) \div 5 =$

**14)** $9 \times 1 + 5 =$

**15)** $2 \times 7 \times 3 =$

**16)** $6 + 4 + 7 =$

**17)** $(10 + 5)^2 =$

**18)** $9 \times 1 \times 7 =$

**19)** $2 \times 10 =$

**20)** $(8^2) \times (9^2) + 1 =$

**21)** $(5 \times 10) - (5 + 9) =$

**22)** $(6 + 4) \times (3 + 9) =$

**23)** $6 \times 9 =$

**24)** $3 + 6 + 3 =$

**25)** $(5^2) \times (4^2) + 5 =$

**26)** $6 + 1 + 10 =$

**27)** $(6 \times 7) - (3 + 7) =$

**28)** $4 + 5^2 + 3 + 1^2 =$

**29)** $8 \times 6 \times 9 =$

**30)** $4(10 + 8) =$

**31)** $5(4 + 5) =$

**32)** $5 + 3 - 10 + 9 =$

**33)** $4 + 4^2 + 1 + 5^2 =$

**34)** $5 \times (4 + 2) =$

**35)** $4 + 8 + 3 + 7 =$

**36)** $(10 + 8)^2 + (3 + 4)^2 =$

**37)** $(2 + 4) \div 2 =$

**38)** $4 + 3 + 4 =$

**39)** $6 + 4^2 + 7 + 6^2 =$

**40)** $(4 + 9) \div 8 =$

**41)** $2 + 9 + 10 =$

**42)** $(3 + 2) \div 2 =$

**43)** $(3^2) \times (4^2) + 3 =$

**44)** $(2^2) \times (9^2) + 2 =$

**45)** $(1^2) \times (7^2) + 1 =$

**46)** $(4 + 2) \div 5 =$

**47)** $(2 + 6) \div 2 =$

**48)** $2 + 2 + 4 =$

**49)** $(10^2) \times (8^2) + 5 =$

**50)** $(8^2) \times (10^2) + 4 =$

**51)** $(10 + 2) \div 6 =$

**52)** $5 \times (3 + 9) =$

**53)** $(3 + 5)^2 =$

**54)** $(9 + 7) \times (1 + 1) =$

**55)** $10 + 2 + 3 + 3 =$

**56)** $2 + 7 + 6 + 1 =$

**57)** $(5 + 2) \div 2 =$

**58)** $(3^2) \times (7^2) + 1 =$

<u>**Solving Equations**</u>

Evaluating expressions involves substituting given values for variables in an expression and then performing the indicated operations to find the result.

For example: Let's evaluate  $4x - 10$, when $x = 3$:

**Step 1: Substitute the given value for the variable:**

Replace every occurrence of x in the expression $4x - 10$ with the given value, which is 3:

$$= 4(3) - 10$$

**Step 2: Perform the operations:**

Perform the indicated operations according to the order of operations (PEMDAS - Parentheses, Exponents, Multiplication and Division, Addition and Subtraction):

$$= 4 \times 3 - 10$$

**Step 3: Simplify:**

Calculate the result:

$$12 - 10 = 2$$

## Solving Equations

Evaluate each expression when: $x = 4$

**1)** $x + 7 + 5x =$

**2)** $2 + (x + 8) =$

**3)** $x + 6 + 5x =$

**4)** $5 + \dfrac{x}{2} =$

**5)** $1 + 3x =$

**6)** $10x^1 + x^1 =$

**7)** $8 \div x =$

**8)** $10 \div (x + 6) =$

**9)** $7x + 5 =$

**10)** $3 - x =$

## Solving Equations

Evaluate each expression when: $x = 4$

**1)** $7 \div (x + 5) =$

**2)** $6 + (x + 2) =$

**3)** $x(5 + x) =$

**4)** $1 + 4x =$

**5)** $8 \div x + 1 =$

**6)** $(5x + 7) + (4x - 4) =$

**7)** $x + 5 =$

**8)** $10x - 1 =$

**9)** $x - 6 =$

**10)** $9 - x =$

NAME: ___________



## Solving Equations

Evaluate each expression when: $x = 4$

**1)** $8x + 6 =$

**2)** $x + 6 + 5x =$

**3)** $x - 8 =$

**4)** $5 - x =$

**5)** $x + x =$

**6)** $10(10 + x) =$

**7)** $x^1 + x - 6 =$

**8)** $9 + 8x =$

**9)** $5x - x =$

**10)** $x + 8 + 2x =$

## Solving Equations

Evaluate each expression when: $x = 2$

**1)** $9 + (x + 9) =$

**2)** $9x + 3 =$

**3)** $3 + 4x =$

**4)** $2x + 3 + (9x - 1) =$

**5)** $9x + 6 =$

**6)** $x + 8 =$

**7)** $x + 1 + 7x =$

**8)** $x - 3 =$

**9)** $x + x =$

**10)** $2 + x =$

NAME: _______________



## Solving Equations

Evaluate each expression when: $x = 7$

**1)** $10x + 2 =$

**2)** $x + 5 =$

**3)** $7x^1 + x^1 =$

**4)** $2x + x - 3 =$

**5)** $x + 5 + 4x =$

**6)** $x + 3 =$

**7)** $x - 6 =$

**8)** $x + 10 =$

**9)** $9^1 + x^1 =$

**10)** $4 + x =$

NAME: ________________



## Solving Equations

Evaluate each expression when: $x = 3$

**1)** $5x + 8x - 1 =$

**2)** $2 + x =$

**3)** $x + 5 =$

**4)** $9 + \dfrac{x}{1} =$

**5)** $x - x =$

**6)** $8x + 2 - 4x =$

**7)** $7x + 9 =$

**8)** $6x - 10 + 6x =$

**9)** $(8x + 2) + (3x - 6) =$

**10)** $6x^1 + 8x^1 =$

## Solving Equations

Evaluate each expression when: $x = 7$

**1)** $9x^1 + 6x^1 =$

**2)** $6x + 6 + (3x - 3) =$

**3)** $2(5x - 9) + 1(3 + x) =$

**4)** $5 + 5x =$

**5)** $4(10 + x) =$

**6)** $5x + 1 =$

**7)** $\dfrac{x}{1} + 4 =$

**8)** $x - 7 =$

**9)** $8x + x =$

**10)** $6x + 7 =$

<u>**Solving Inequalities**</u>

Inequalities are mathematical expressions that compare the relative sizes of two values. They are used to express relationships where one quantity is:

- "<" (less than),
- ">" (greater than),
- "<=" (less than or equal to),
- ">=" (greater than or equal to),
- and "≠" (not equal to) another quantity.

For example:

$$y + \text{-}10 \leq -8$$

To isolate $y$, we need to get rid of the constant term $-10$. Since $-10$ is being subtracted from $y$, we can undo this operation by adding 10 to both sides of the inequality:

$$y - 10 + 10 \leq -8 + 10$$

$$y \leq 2$$

To check the solution:

$$2 - 10 \leq -8$$

$$-8 = -8$$

The inequality is true when $y = 2$

## Solving Inequalities

**1)**

$$-6 < -8 + y$$

**2)**

$$z - 3 > 7$$

**3)**

$$-16 \leq -24z$$

**4)**

$$\frac{m}{7} \leq -7$$

**5)**

$$6x > 2$$

**6)**

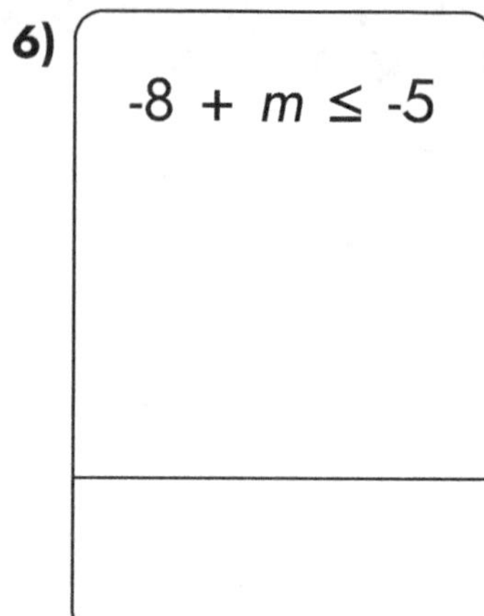

$$-8 + m \leq -5$$

**7)**

$$-3 - z \geq -1$$

**8)**

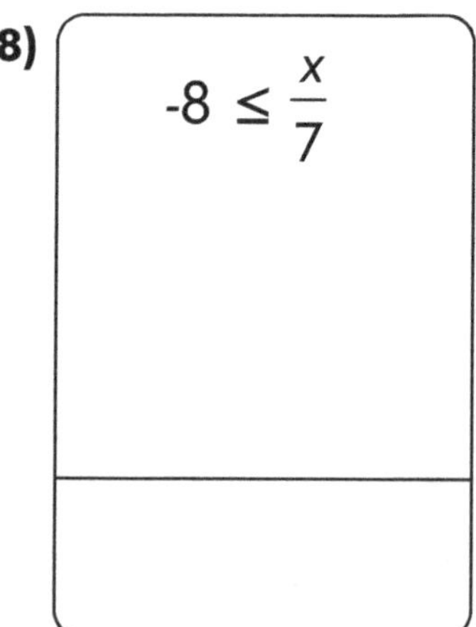

$$-8 \leq \frac{x}{7}$$

**9)**

$$15x \geq -9$$

**10)**

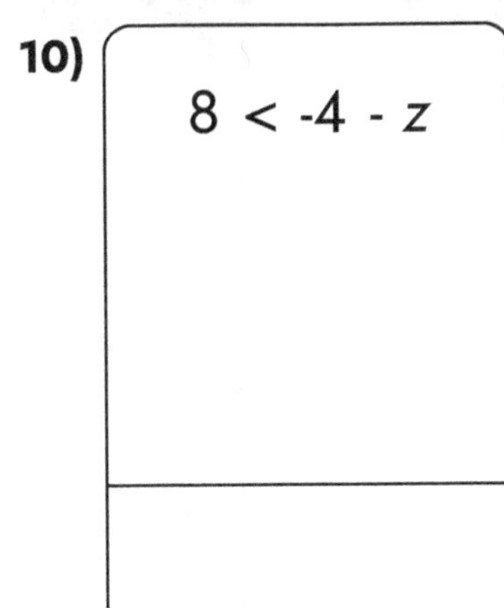

$$8 < -4 - z$$

**11)**

$$3 + z \geq 3$$

**12)**

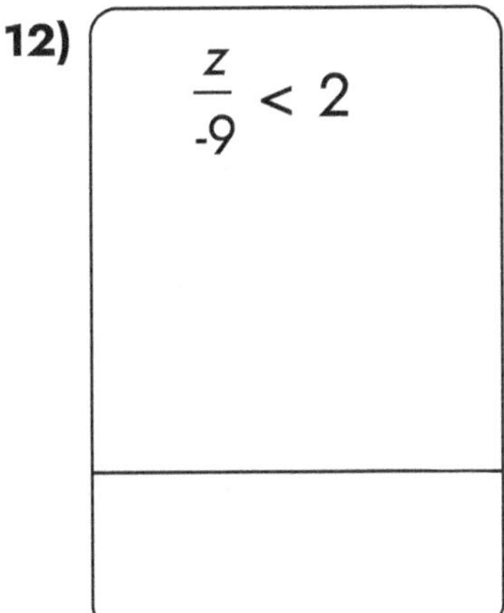

$$\frac{z}{-9} < 2$$

**13)**

$$-8 < 7 + y$$

**14)**

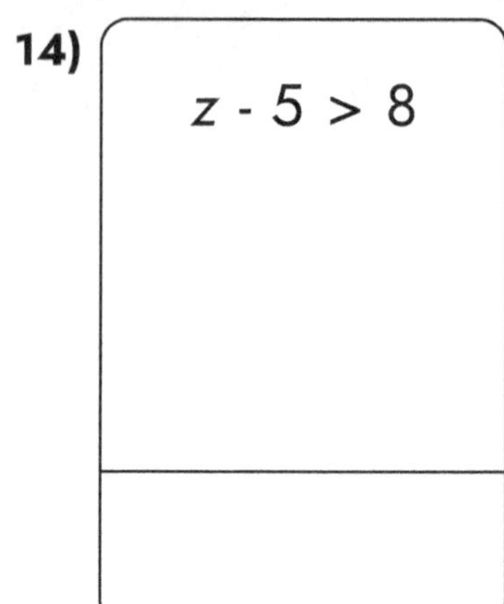

$$z - 5 > 8$$

**15)**

$$-8 > \frac{x}{1}$$

**16)**

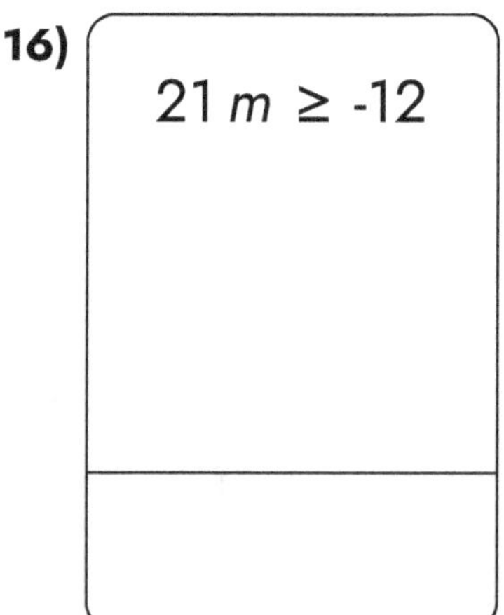

$$21\,m \geq -12$$

**17)**

$m - 7 \leq 8$

**18)**

$-12x < -9$

**19)**

$\dfrac{x}{-7} \geq 5$

**20)**

$x + -4 \leq -10$

**21)**

$$8 \geq m + -7$$

**22)**

$$y - -2 \geq 9$$

**23)**

$$2m \geq -4$$

**24)**

$$3 \geq \frac{x}{-4}$$

**25)**

$$-5 - m \geq -2$$

**26)** 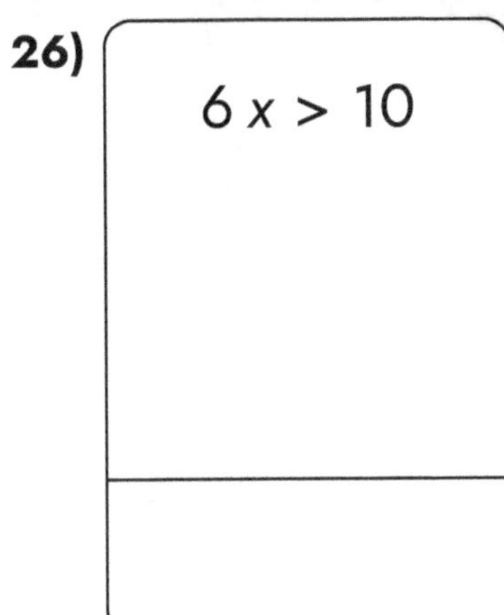

$$6x > 10$$

**27)**

$$-9 < \frac{m}{-5}$$

**28)** 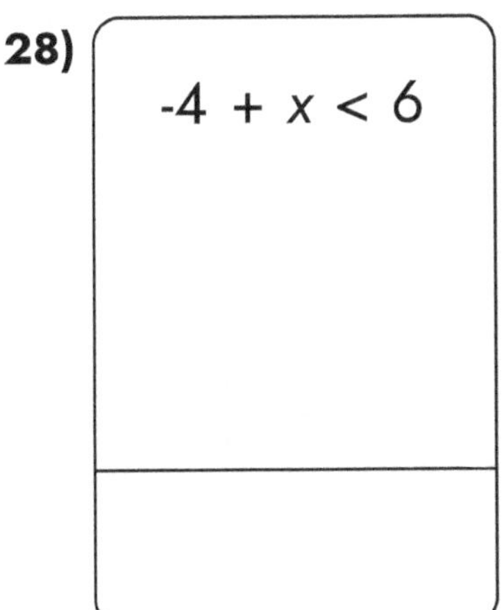

$$-4 + x < 6$$

**29)**

$$-6 < \frac{y}{4}$$

**30)**

$$3 \leq m + 1$$

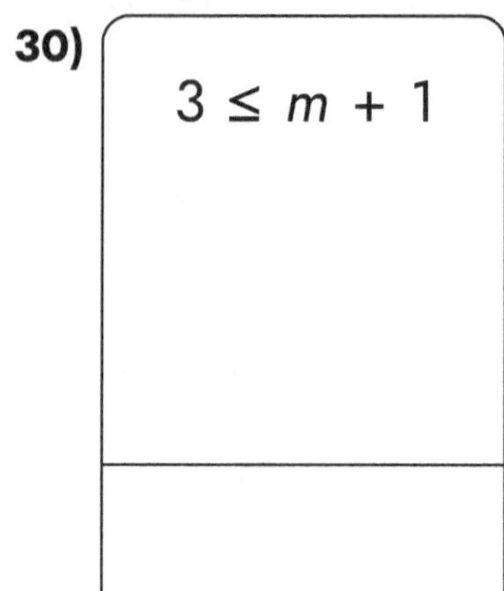

**31)**

$$9\,k \geq 15$$

**32)**

$$-7 - x > -6$$

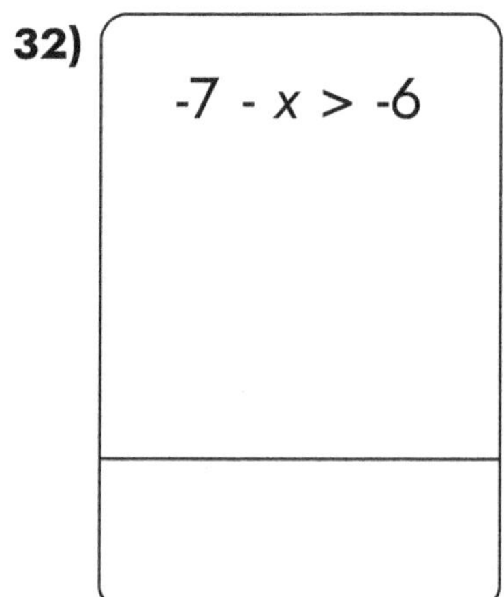

**33)**

$$-8 < y + 2$$

**34)**

$$0 \geq y - -6$$

**35)**

$$-9 < \dfrac{x}{-4}$$

**36)**

$$4 \leq -10\,k$$

**37)**

$$-8 \leq 9 + k$$

**38)**

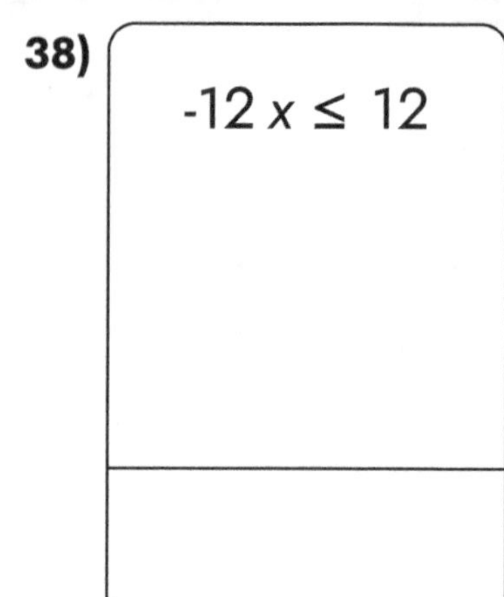

$$-12x \leq 12$$

**39)**

$$7 \leq \frac{k}{-5}$$

**40)**

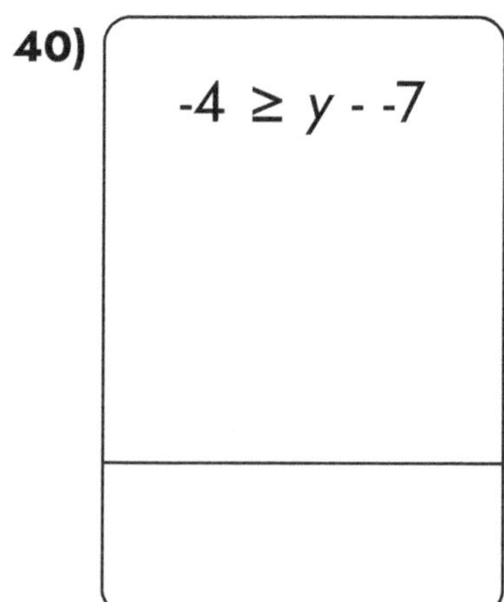

$$-4 \geq y - -7$$

<u>**Simplifying Expressions**</u>

It involves combining like terms and performing operations to make the expression easier to understand and work with.

Let's simplify the expression:

$$2x - 2x + 8 + 4$$

- Combine like terms: First, we look for terms with the same variable and exponent. In this expression, $2x$ and $-2x$ are like terms, so they can be combined:

$$2x - 2x = 0$$

- Substitute the simplified terms: After combining the like terms, the expression becomes:

$$0 + 8 + 4$$

- Combine the remaining terms: Now, we add the constants together:

$$8 + 4 = 12$$

## Simplify Expressions

**1)** $18x - 10x$

**2)** $13m - 3 - 18m + 16 - 20$

**3)** $15 - 18(-20y + 16)$

**4)** $16 + 8y - 16 + y - 20 + 5y$

**5)** $3k + 2 + 5k$

**6)** $11m + m$

**7)** $-12 + 14 - 10y + 6y - 10 + 19y$

**8)** $6y - y$

**9)** $19x + 8 - 5x - 19 + 11x - 14$

**10)** $19x - 4 - 10x + 18$

**11)** $11k - 20k + 16k - 14 + 17$

**12)** $19 + 15z - 8 + 8z$

**13)** $x + 7 - 3x - 11 + 2x - 13$

**14)** $-10y - 11 + 1 - 9y$

**15)** $-11x + 16 + 2x + 14 + 9x - 9$

**16)** $9m + m$

**17)** $-2 - 11z + 7z - 10 + 18z$

**18)** $13 + 13x - 11 + 13x$

**19)** $12 - 7y + 11 - 12y + 9 - 4y$

**20)** $-m + m$

**21)** $15 - 10x + 10 - 19x + 10 - 9x$

**22)** $18 + 16m - 7 + 15m$

**23)** $19y - 20 - 4y + 6 - 17$

**24)** $m + 20 + m$

**25)** $17 + 19(-20x + 18)$

**26)** $-4z + 6 - 10z$

**27)** $-x - 6x$

**28)** $-x - 8x$

**29)** $-7k + 4 - 12k$

**30)** $8 + m - 16 + 18m$

**31)** $-17k - 19 - 13k$

**32)** $20 + 8(-7z + 12)$

33) $-3 - 15m + 18 - 12m$

34) $-8y + 1 + 6y + 9 + 13y - 7$

35) $-19x - 4 - 12x$

36) $k - 1 - 15k + 9 - 1$

37) $-15 + 5z - 3z - 16 - 10z$

38) $-6z + 13z + 20 - 3z$

39) $15x + 18x$

40) $-7z - 1 + 17z$

41) $9 + 7k - 2k + 3 - 12k$

42) $-18k + 15 - 2k$

43) $y - 20y + 6y + 13 + 4$

44) $y + 1 + 17y$

45) $18z - 12 - 13z + 16$

46) $2 + 16x - 4x + 5 - 19x$

47) $7y + 11 - 9y + 5 + 6y + 2$

48) $6z + 2z$

<u>**Linear Functions**</u>

A linear equation is an algebraic equation that represents a straight line when graphed on a coordinate plane. It consists of variables raised to the power of 1 (i.e., no exponents higher than 1) and constant coefficients.

The general form of a linear equation in one variable x is:

$$ax + b = 0$$

Where $a$ and $b$ are constants, and $x$ is the variable.

Let's solve the linear equation:

$$-2x + 9 = 5$$

- **Isolate the variable term:** We want to isolate the term containing $x$ on one side of the equation. To do this, we'll move the constant term to the other side. Subtract 9 from both sides:

$$-2x + 9 - 9 = 5 - 9$$

$$-2x = -4$$

- **Divide by the coefficient of the variable:** To solve for $x$, divide both sides by the coefficient of $x$, which is -2:

$$\frac{-2x}{-2} = \frac{-4}{-2}$$

$$x = 2$$

## Linear Equations

Solve for the variable.

**1)** $9(2x - 9) = -45$

**2)** $2x + 1 = -7$

**3)** $-8y + 6y = -16$

**4)** $8y + 3y - 6 = -83$

**5)** $10(-7y - 4) = -530$

**6)** $x + 0 = 6$

**7)** $-7(6y - 2) = -280$

**8)** $-4x + (-6)x - 1 = -101$

9) $3x + (-10)x = 28$

10) $-5y + (-7)y - 9 = 51$

11) $5y + 10y - (-8) = -127$

12) $2y + 0 = 0$

13) $5(-1y - 9) = -5$

14) $6x = 42$

15) $-6y - (-3) = -57$

16) $0x + 3x - 6 = -21$

**17)** $6(6x - (-4)) = -84$

**18)** $-4y = 16$

**19)** $x + (-1) = -6$

**20)** $7y = 56$

**21)** $-3(2x - (-2)) = 54$

**22)** $5(4y - (-6)) = -10$

**23)** $-10y + (-10)y - (-2) = -58$

**24)** $-1x + (-6) = -3$

<u>**Slop from Two Points**</u>

The slope between two points on a Cartesian coordinate system is a measure of the steepness of the line connecting those points. It's calculated by finding the change in the y-coordinates divided by the change in the x-coordinates.

- The coordinates of the first point as $(x1, y1) = (2, -30)$.

- The coordinates of the second point as $(x2, y2) = (-5, 40)$.

The formula to calculate the slope ($m$) between two points:

$$\frac{y2 - y1}{x2 - x1}$$

## Find Slope from two Points

**1)** (7, -17 ) and (-18 , 6 )

**2)** (-16, 10 ) and (-5 , 15 )

**3)** (17, -16 ) and (19 , -12 )

**4)** (5, 1 ) and (-7 , 14 )

**5)** (10, -11 ) and (15 , -2 )

**6)** (-20, -19 ) and (3 , 17 )

**7)** (-18, -3 ) and (10 , 11 )

**8)** (-12, 12 ) and (-19 , 2 )

**9)** (3, -3 ) and (-10 , -3 )

**10)** (18, 18 ) and (-9 , -3 )

**11)** (4, 15 ) and (10 , 9 )

**12)** (-7, 10 ) and (4 , 11 )

**13)** (-9, -3 ) and (14 , 18 )

**14)** (18, -7 ) and (-12 , 6 )

**15)** (1, -15 ) and (4 , 7 )

**16)** (20, 4 ) and (7 , -15 )

**17)** (-17, -4 ) and (5 , -12 )

**18)** (-10, 16 ) and (16 , 12 )

**19)** (19, -2 ) and (14 , -14 )

**20)** (-9, 15 ) and (4 , -7 )

**21)** (14, 19 ) and (0 , 12 )

**22)** (18, -17 ) and (5 , -11 )

**23)** (-11, 5 ) and (17 , 13 )

**24)** (-6, 4 ) and (-3 , -20 )

<u>**Graphing Linear Equation**</u>

Graphing a linear equation involves plotting the points that satisfy the equation on a coordinate plane and connecting them to form a straight line. Linear equations are equations of the form $y = mx + b$, where $m$ represents the slope of the line, and $b$ represents the y-intercept, the point where the line intersects the y-axis.

To graph a linear equation:

1. Identify the slope ($m$) and y-intercept ($b$) from the equation.

2. Plot the y-intercept $(0, b))$ as a point on the y-axis.

3. Use the slope to find additional points on the line. The slope represents the change in y for every unit change in x.

4. Connect the points to form a straight line.

For example, to graph the equation:

$$y = \frac{9}{4}x - 8$$

1. **Identify the slope and y-intercept:** The slope is $\frac{9}{4}$, and the y-intercept is −8.

2. **Plot the y-intercept:** Plot the point $(0, -8)$.

3. **Use the slope to plot additional points:** the slop is $\frac{9}{4}$ to find another point. we will move up 9 units and 4 units to the right from the y-intercept to find another point.

4. **Draw the line:** Once we have at least two points, we can draw a straight line.

We can continue this process to plot more points and extend the line further if needed.

$$y = \frac{9}{4}x - 8$$

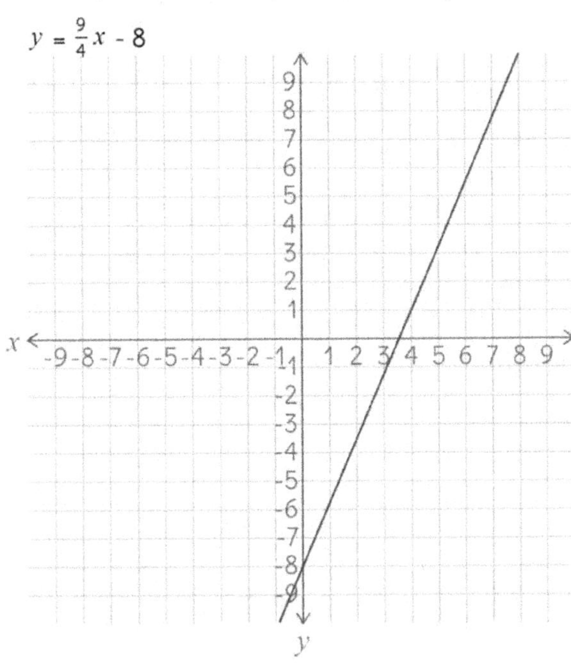

## Graphing Linear Equations

1) 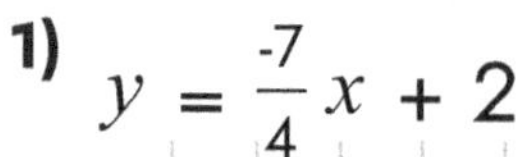

$$y = \frac{-7}{4}x + 2$$

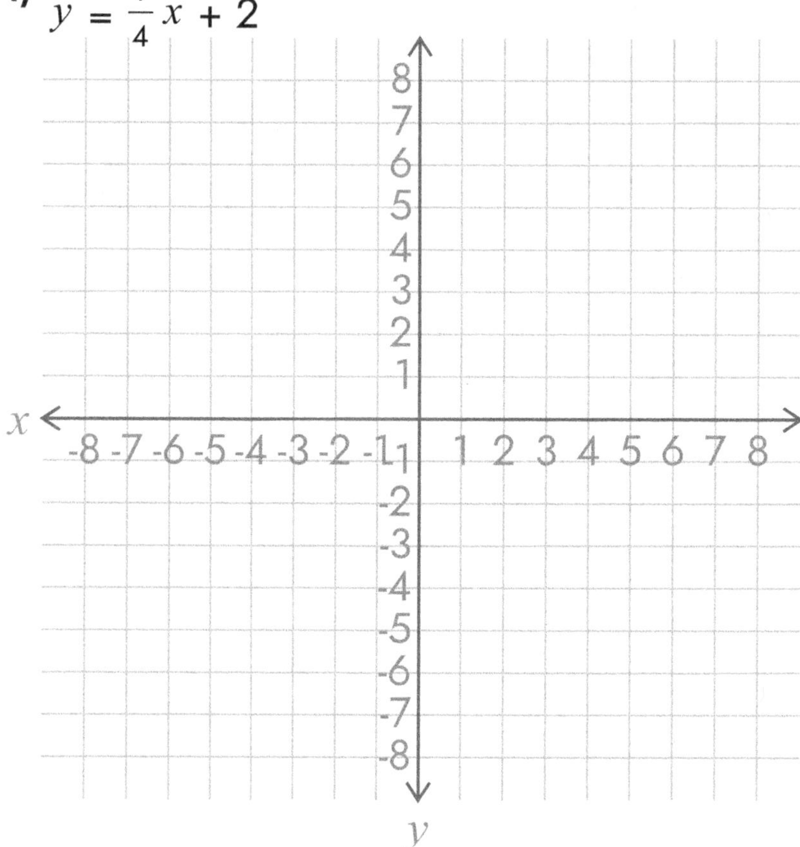

**2)** $y = x + 7$

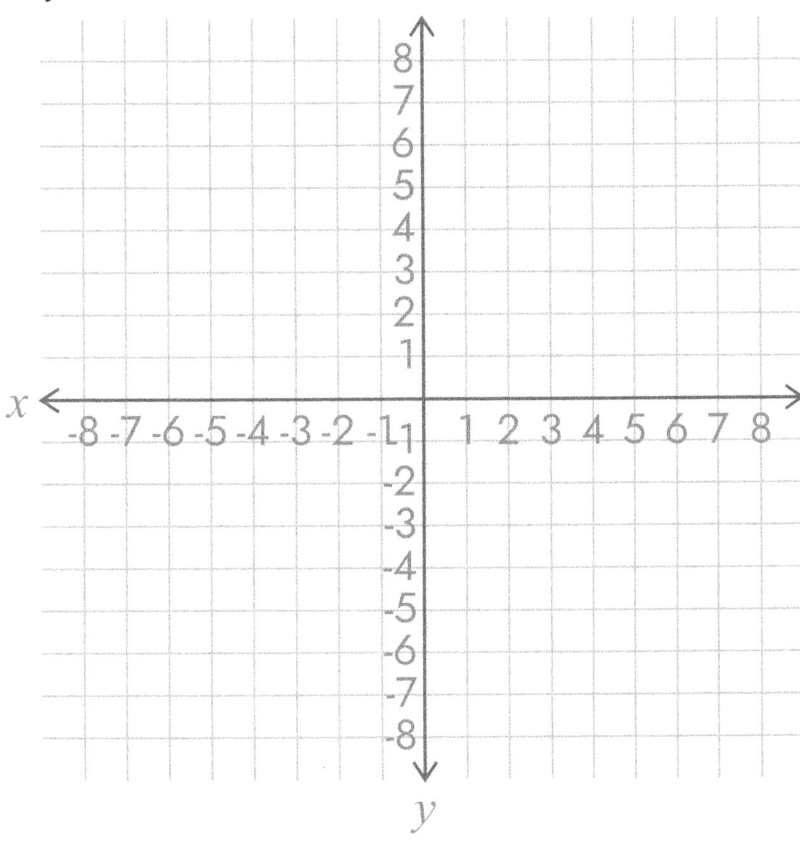

**3)** $y = \dfrac{-9}{4}x - 2$

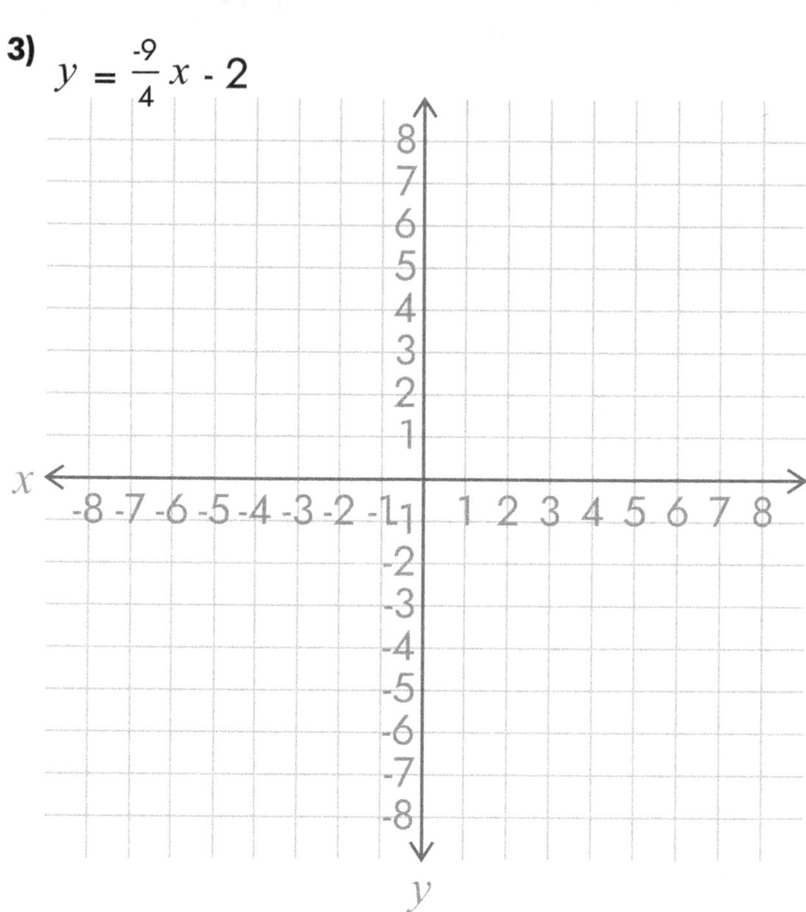

**4)** $y = -2$

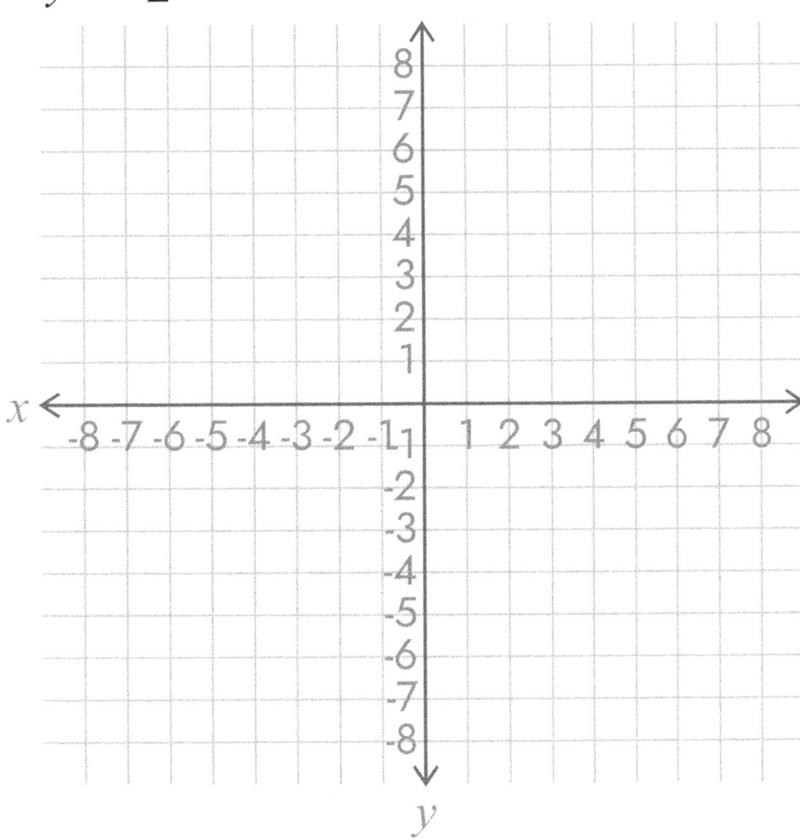

**5)** $y = \dfrac{1}{4}x - 8$

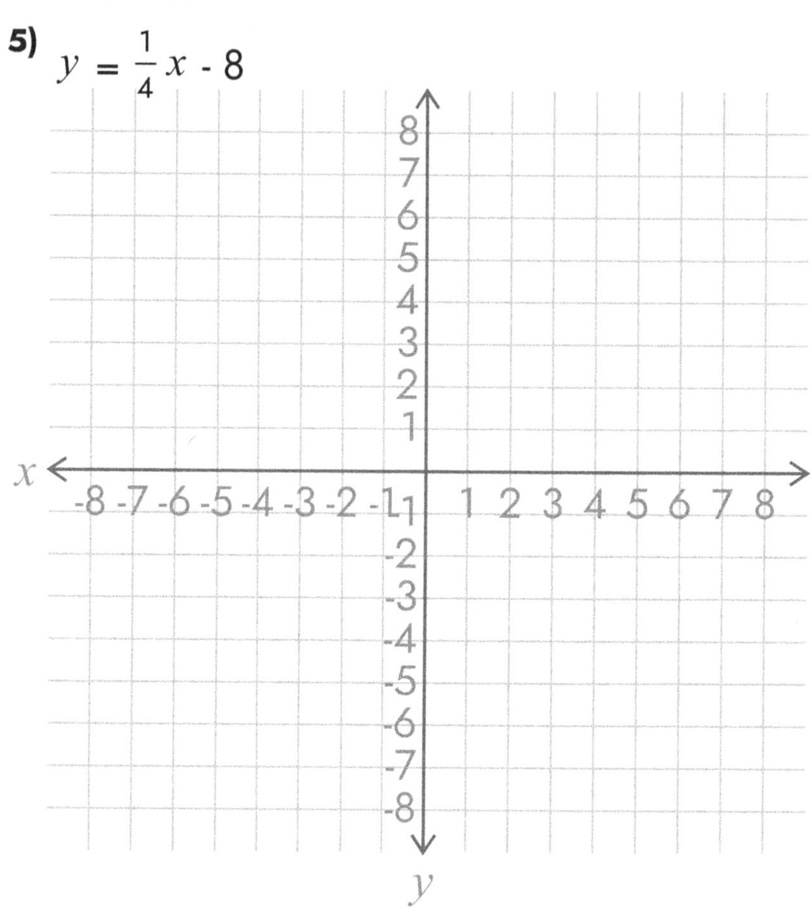

# System of Equations

A system of equations is a collection of two or more equations involving the same set of variables. The solution to a system of equations is the set of values for the variables that satisfy all the equations simultaneously.

## Solving by Elimination:

To solve a system of equations by elimination, we manipulate the equations to eliminate one of the variables.

Given the system:

$$4x + 5y = 6$$

$$10x + 6y = 8$$

Step 1: Multiply each equation by a constant such that the coefficients of one of the variables become equal or multiples of each other.

Let's try to eliminate the variable $x$.

- Multiply the first equation by 5 and the second equation by -2:

$$20x + 25y = 30$$

$$-20x - 12y = -16$$

Step 2: Add the two equations together to eliminate the variable $x$:

$$(20x - 20x) + (25y - 12y) = 30 - 16$$

$$13y = 14$$

Step 3: Solve for $y$:

$$y = \frac{14}{13} = 1.077$$

Step 4: Substitute the value of y into one of the original equations to solve for x. Let's use the first equation:

$$4x + 5\left(\frac{14}{13}\right) = 6$$

$$4x + \frac{70}{13} = 6$$

$$4x = 6 - \frac{70}{13}$$

$$4x = \frac{78 - 70}{13}$$

$$4x = \frac{8}{13}$$

$$x = \frac{2}{13} = 0.154$$

the solution to the system of equations is x =0.154 and y = 1.077.

## System of Equations

1. $2x + 2y = 7$

   $6x + 10y = 1$

2. $8x + 9y = 3$

   $5x + 5y = 3$

3. $4x + 3y = 3$

   $9x + 4y = 10$

4. $10x + 6y = 2$

   $2x + 2y = 1$

5. $5x + 2y = 9$

   $9x + 5y = 3$

6. $8x + 9y = 10$

   $6x + 5y = 1$

7. $9x + 6y = 6$

$5x + 4y = 10$

8. $8x + 3y = 6$

$5x + 10y = 8$

9. $3x + 2y = 2$

$2x + 1y = 5$

10. $3x + 8y = 8$

   $7x + 1y = 7$

11. $7x + 6y = 1$

   $1x + 1y = 5$

12. $4x + 2y = 4$

   $10x + 7y = 9$

13. $1x + 2y = 1$

$9x + 5y = 1$

14. $6x + 4y = 3$

$7x + 3y = 9$

15. $6x + 7y = 9$

$7x + 2y = 1$

16. $5x + 4y = 5$

    $10x + 7y = 3$

17. $3x + 5y = 4$

    $5x + 4y = 9$

18. $8x + 1y = 10$

    $7x + 2y = 3$

19. $8x + 4y = 8$

    $3x + 1y = 10$

20. $4x + 5y = 9$

    $6x + 4y = 8$

<u>**Quadratic Equations**</u>

A quadratic equation is a polynomial equation of the second degree, meaning it can be written in the form:

$$ax^2 + bx + c = 0$$

where a, b, and c are constants, and x is the variable being solved for. The solutions to a quadratic equation are the values of x that make the equation true.

Now, let's solve the quadratic equation $11x^2 - 1 = 0$ and understand it step by step using quadratic formula.

1. Identify the coefficients:
   In the equation $11x^2 - 1 = 0$,
$$a=11,\ b=0,\ \text{and}\ c=-1.$$
2. Apply the quadratic formula:
   The quadratic formula states that for an equation $ax^2 + bx + c = 0$, the solutions for x are given by:
$$x = \frac{-b \pm \sqrt{b^2 - 4ac}}{2a}$$

   Plugging in the values a=11, b=0, and c=−1 into the quadratic formula, we get:
$$x = \frac{-0 \pm \sqrt{0 - 4(11)(-1)}}{2(11)}$$
3. Simplify inside the square root:

$$0^2 - 4(11)\,(-1) = 0 - (-44) = 44$$

4. Plug in the simplified values:
$$x = \frac{\pm \sqrt{44}}{22}$$
5. Simplify the square root:
   Since 44 is not a perfect square, we can write it as $\sqrt[2]{11}$

$$x = \frac{\pm \sqrt[2]{11}}{22}$$

6. Simplify further if possible:

   We can simplify $\sqrt[2]{11}$ to $\sqrt{11}$ by canceling out the common factor:

$$x = \frac{\pm \sqrt{11}}{11}$$

7. Final solution:

   So, the solutions to the equation are:

$$x = \frac{\sqrt{11}}{11} \text{ and } x = \frac{-\sqrt{11}}{11}$$

$$\text{or}$$

$$(x = 0.302, \text{ and } x = -0.302)$$

These are the roots of the quadratic equation. They represent the points where the graph of the quadratic equation intersects the x-axis.

Let's solve another equation:

$$-4p^2 + 6p - 6 = 0$$

$$p = \frac{-b \pm \sqrt{b^2 - 4ac}}{2a}$$

where $a = -4$, $b = 6$, and $c = -6$.

Let's plug these values into the quadratic formula:

$$p = \frac{-6 \pm \sqrt{6^2 - 4(-4)(-6)}}{2(-4)}$$

First, let's simplify inside the square root:

$$6^2 - 4\,(-4)\,(-6)$$

$$= 36 - 96 = -60$$

So, we have:

$$p = \frac{-6 \pm \sqrt{-60}}{-8}$$

We can simplify the square root of $-60$ by factoring out $-1$:

$$\sqrt{-60}$$

$$= \sqrt{-1 \times 60}$$

$$= \sqrt{-1} \times \sqrt{60}$$

$$= i\sqrt{60}$$

So, we have:

$$p = \frac{-6 \pm i\sqrt{60}}{-8}$$

Simplify:

$$\sqrt{60} \text{ to } \sqrt{4 \times 15} = 2\sqrt{15}$$

$$p = \frac{-6 \pm i \times 2\sqrt{15}}{-8}$$

Now, divide both the numerator and denominator by −2 to simplify:

$$p = \frac{3 \pm i\sqrt{15}}{4}$$

So, the solutions to the equation are:

$$p = \frac{3 + i\sqrt{15}}{4} \text{ and } p = \frac{3 - i\sqrt{15}}{4}$$

This equation $-4p^2 + 6p - 6 = 0$ has no real solutions.

When a quadratic equation has no real solutions, it means that the solutions are not real numbers, but rather complex numbers. In this case, the solutions involve the imaginary unit $i$ because the discriminant ($b^2 - 4ac$) is negative, which results in taking the square root of a negative number when applying the quadratic formula.

In mathematics, such equations are said to have "no real roots" or "no real solutions." They are also sometimes referred to as having "complex roots" or "complex solutions." Complex numbers include a real part and an imaginary part, and they are often written in the form $a + bi$, where $a$ and $b$ are real numbers and $i$ is the imaginary unit, defined as $i = \sqrt{-1}$.

Let's solve another equation:

$$12x^2 + 6x - 2 = 0$$

$$x = \frac{-b \pm \sqrt{b^2 - 4ac}}{2a}$$

where $a = 12$, $b = 6$, and $c = -2$.

Let's plug these values into the quadratic formula:

$$x = \frac{-6 \pm \sqrt{6^2 - 4(12)(-2)}}{2(12)}$$

First, let's simplify inside the square root:

$$6^2 - 4(12)(-2)$$
$$= 36 - (-96)$$
$$= 36 + 96$$
$$= 132$$

So, we have:

$$x = \frac{-6 \pm \sqrt{132}}{24}$$

Now, let's simplify the square root of 132:

$$x = \frac{-6 \pm \sqrt{4 \times 33}}{24}$$
$$x = \frac{-6 \pm 2\sqrt{33}}{24}$$
$$x = \frac{-6 \pm \sqrt{33}}{12}$$

So, the solutions to the equation are:

$$x = \frac{-6 + \sqrt{33}}{12} \text{ and } x = \frac{-6 - \sqrt{33}}{12}$$

or $(x = 0.229$, and $x = -0.729)$

Let's solve a quadratic equation where the right side is a number, instead of 0.

$$-8n^2 + 6n + 30 = 7$$

To solve the equation, we first need to bring all terms to one side to set the equation equal to zero:

$$-8n^2 + 6n + 30 - 7 = 0$$

Simplify:

$$-8n^2 + 6n + 23 = 0$$

Now, to solve for n, we can use the quadratic formula:

$$n = \frac{-b \pm \sqrt{b^2 - 4ac}}{2a}$$

where $a = -8$, $b = 6$, and $c = 23$.

Plugging these values into the formula, we get:

$$n = \frac{-6 \pm \sqrt{6^2 - 4(-8)(23)}}{2(-8)}$$

$$n = \frac{-6 \pm \sqrt{36 + 736}}{-16}$$

$$n = \frac{-6 \pm \sqrt{772}}{-16}$$

Now, let's simplify the square root of 772. We can factor out 4:

$$\sqrt{772} = \sqrt{4 \times 193} = 2\sqrt{193}$$

So, our equation becomes:

$$n = \frac{-6 \pm 2\sqrt{193}}{-8}$$

So, the solutions to the equation are:

$$n = \frac{-3 + \sqrt{193}}{-8} \text{ and } n = \frac{-3 - \sqrt{193}}{-8}$$

*or*

$$(n = -1.362, \text{ and } n = 2.112)$$

## Quadratic Equations

**1.** $-10r^2 - 11r - 9 = 0$

**2.** $-11k^2 + 9 = 0$

**3.** $11x^2 + 4x - 16 = 0$

**4.** $x^2 - x - 90 = 0$

**5.** $9n^2 - 8n - 11 = 0$

**6.** $n^2 + 11n + 30 = 0$

**7.** $6n^2 - 8n - 14 = 0$

**10.** $3v^2 - 12v - 63 = 0$

**8.** $-6v^2 + 6 = 0$

**11.** $7p^2 - 6p - 4 = 8$

**9.** $3n^2 - 2n - 1 = 0$

**12.** $-5x^2 - 7x + 24 = 12$

**13.** $-m^2 + 8 = -8$

**16.** $x^2 + 11x = -30$

**14.** $7v^2 - 5v - 3 = -6$

**17.** $-11m^2 + 22 = -9m$

**15.** $-4k^2 + 117 = -4$

**18.** $-4n^2 + 36 = 0$

# ANSWERS

### Page 1:   Equations (One Side)

| | | | | | |
|---|---|---|---|---|---|
| **1.** $y = 10$ | **2.** $z = 7$ | **3.** $z = 8$ | **4.** $k = 1$ | **5.** $k = 8$ | **6.** $k = 3$ |
| **7.** $x = 3$ | **8.** $z = 6$ | **9.** $y = 2$ | **10.** $k = 6$ | **11.** $z = 8$ | **12.** $y = 10$ |
| **13.** $m = 4$ | **14.** $y = 10$ | **15.** $x = 8$ | **16.** $z = 8$ | **17.** $z = 3$ | **18.** $m = 15$ |
| **19.** $m = 4$ | **20.** $m = 3$ | **21.** $m = 5$ | **22.** $m = 9$ | **23.** $k = 5$ | **24.** $m = 9$ |
| **25.** $m = 8$ | **26.** $m = 2$ | **27.** $m = 4$ | **28.** $k = 6$ | **29.** $y = 1$ | **30.** $m = 10$ |
| **31.** $z = 10$ | **32.** $z = 9$ | **33.** $m = 9$ | **34.** $m = 5$ | **35.** $x = 6$ | **36.** $k = 20$ |
| **37.** $y = 10$ | **38.** $x = 1$ | **39.** $z = 6$ | **40.** $m = 9$ | **41.** $x = 1$ | **42.** $y = 5$ |
| **43.** $z = 8$ | **44.** $m = 8$ | **45.** $k = 4$ | **46.** $y = 10$ | **47.** $x = 2$ | **48.** $z = 7$ |
| **49.** $z = 1$ | **50.** $k = 7$ | | | | |

### Page 6:   Equations (Two Sides)

| | | | | | | |
|---|---|---|---|---|---|---|
| **1.** $m = 4$ | **2.** $y = 8$ | **3.** $y = 1$ | **4.** $y = 4$ | **5.** $x = 5$ | **6.** $z = 2$ | **7.** $y = 1$ |
| **8.** $k = 6$ | **9.** $k = 9$ | **10.** $y = 6$ | **11.** $z = 9$ | **12.** $z = 9$ | **13.** $z = 8$ | **14.** $z = 9$ |
| **15.** $m = 4$ | **16.** $z = 2$ | **17.** $k = 1$ | **18.** $y = 4$ | **19.** $m = 8$ | **20.** $k = 4$ | **21.** $z = 3$ |
| **22.** $x = 6$ | **23.** $m = 3$ | **24.** $z = 4$ | **25.** $x = 7$ | **26.** $m = 3$ | **27.** $m = 7$ | **28.** $x = 9$ |
| **29.** $m = 4$ | **30.** $y = 5$ | **31.** $x = 9$ | **32.** $x = 5$ | **33.** $y = 7$ | **34.** $x = 7$ | **35.** $y = 1$ |
| **36.** $z = 6$ | **37.** $m = 7$ | **38.** $y = 9$ | **39.** $m = 5$ | **40.** $k = 5$ | **41.** $x = 8$ | **42.** $k = 5$ |
| **43.** $k = 1$ | **44.** $y = 3$ | **45.** $k = 1$ | **46.** $m = 5$ | **47.** $m = 3$ | **48.** $y = 2$ | |

### Page 11:   Order of Operations (PEMDAS)

| | | | | | |
|---|---|---|---|---|---|
| **1.** 20 | **2.** 266 | **3.** 52 | **4.** 2 | **5.** 4 | **6.** 2 |

| | | | | | |
|---|---|---|---|---|---|
| **7.** 288 | **8.** 44 | **9.** 120 | **10.** 33 | **11.** 19 | **12.** -9 |
| **13.** 2.8 | **14.** 14 | **15.** 42 | **16.** 17 | **17.** 225 | **18.** 63 |
| **19.** 20 | **20.** 5,185 | **21.** 36 | **22.** 120 | **23.** 54 | **24.** 12 |
| **25.** 405 | **26.** 17 | **27.** 32 | **28.** 33 | **29.** 432 | **30.** 72 |
| **31.** 45 | **32.** 7 | **33.** 46 | **34.** 30 | **35.** 22 | **36.** 373 |
| **37.** 3 | **38.** 11 | **39.** 65 | **40.** 1.6 | **41.** 21 | **42.** 2.5 |
| **43.** 147 | **44.** 326 | **45.** 50 | **46.** 1.2 | **47.** 4 | **48.** 8 |
| **49.** 6,405 | **50.** 6,404 | **51.** 2 | **52.** 60 | **53.** 64 | **54.** 32 |
| **55.** 18 | **56.** 16 | **57.** 3.5 | **58.** 442 | | |

**Page 17:  Solving Equations**

**1.** 31   **2.** 14   **3.** 30   **4.** 7   **5.** 13   **6.** 44   **7.** 2   **8.** 1   **9.** 33   **10.** -1

**Page 18:  Solving Equations**

**1.** 0.8   **2.** 12   **3.** 36   **4.** 17   **5.** 3   **6.** 39   **7.** 9   **8.** 39   **9.** -2   **10.** 5

**Page 19:  Solving Equations**

**1.** 38   **2.** 30   **3.** -4   **4.** 1   **5.** 8   **6.** 140   **7.** 2   **8.** 41   **9.** 16

**10.** 20

**Page 20:  Solving Equations**

**1.** 20   **2.** 21   **3.** 11   **4.** 24   **5.** 24   **6.** 10   **7.** 17   **8.** -1   **9.** 4   **10.** 4

**Page 21:  Solving Equations**

**1.** 72   **2.** 12   **3.** 56   **4.** 18   **5.** 40   **6.** 10   **7.** 1   **8.** 17   **9.** 16   **10.** 11

**Page 22:  Solving Equations**

**1.** 38   **2.** 5   **3.** 8   **4.** 12   **5.** 0   **6.** 14   **7.** 30   **8.** 26   **9.** 29   **10.** 42

**Page 23:    Solving Equations**

**1.** 105    **2.** 66    **3.** 62    **4.** 40    **5.** 68    **6.** 36    **7.** 11    **8.** 0    **9.** 63    **10.** 49

**Page 24:    Solving Inequalities**

**1.** $y > 2$    **2.** $z > 10$    **3.** $z \geq 2/3$    **4.** $m \leq -49$    **5.** $x > 1/3$

**6.** $m \leq 3$    **7.** $z \geq -2$    **8.** $x \geq -56$    **9.** $x \geq -3/5$    **10.** $z > -12$

**11.** $z \geq 0$    **12.** $z < -18$    **13.** $y > -15$    **14.** $z > 13$    **15.** $x < -8$

**16.** $m \geq -4/7$    **17.** $m \leq 15$    **18.** $x < 3/4$    **19.** $x \geq -35$    **20.** $x \leq -6$

**21.** $m \leq 15$    **22.** $y \geq 7$    **23.** $m \geq -2$    **24.** $x \leq -12$    **25.** $m \geq -3$

**26.** $x > 5/3$    **27.** $m > 45$    **28.** $x < 10$    **29.** $y > -24$    **30.** $m \geq 2$

**31.** $k \geq 5/3$    **32.** $x > -1$    **33.** $y > -10$    **34.** $y \leq -6$    **35.** $x > 36$

**36.** $k \geq -2/5$    **37.** $k \geq -17$    **38.** $x \leq -1$    **39.** $k \geq -35$    **40.** $y \leq -11$

**Page 34:    Simplify Expressions**

**1.** $8x$    **2.** $-5m - 7$    **3.** $360y - 273$    **4.** $14y - 20$

**5.** $8k + 2$    **6.** $12m$    **7.** $15y - 8$    **8.** $5y$

**9.** $25x - 25$    **10.** $9x + 14$    **11.** $7k + 3$    **12.** $23z + 11$

**13.** $-17$    **14.** $-19y - 10$    **15.** $21$    **16.** $10m$

**17.** $14z - 12$    **18.** $26x + 2$    **19.** $-23y + 32$    **20.** $0$

**21.** $-38x + 35$    **22.** $31m + 11$    **23.** $15y - 31$    **24.** $2m + 20$

**25.** $-380x + 359$    **26.** $-14z + 6$    **27.** $-7x$    **28.** $-9x$

**29.** $-19k + 4$    **30.** $19m - 8$    **31.** $-30k - 19$    **32.** $-56z + 116$

**33.** $-27m + 15$    **34.** $11y + 3$    **35.** $-31x - 4$    **36.** $-14k + 7$

**37.** $-8z - 31$    **38.** $4z + 20$    **39.** $33x$    **40.** $10z - 1$

**41.** −7k + 12      **42.** −20k + 15      **43.** −13y + 17      **44.** 18y + 1

**45.** 5z + 4      **46.** −7x + 7      **47.** 4y + 18      **48.** 8z

## Page 40:  Linear Equations

**1.** 2      **2.** -4      **3.** 8      **4.** -7      **5.** 7      **6.** 6      **7.** 7      **8.** 10      **9.** -4

**10.** -5      **11.** -9      **12.** 0      **13.** -8      **14.** 7      **15.** 10      **16.** -5      **17.** -3      **18.** -4

**19.** -5      **20.** 8      **21.** -10      **22.** -2      **23.** 3      **24.** -3

## Page 43:  Find Slope from two Points

**1.** -0.92      **2.** 0.45      **3.** 2      **4.** -1.08      **5.** 1.8      **6.** 1.57      **7.** 0.5

**8.** 1.43      **9.** 0      **10.** 0.78      **11.** -1      **12.** 0.09      **13.** 0.91      **14.** -0.43

**15.** 7.33      **16.** 1.46      **17.** -0.36      **18.** -0.15      **19.** 2.4      **20.** -1.69      **21.** 0.5

**22.** -0.46      **23.** 0.29      **24.** -8

## Page 46:  Graphing Linear Equations

**1.** $y = \frac{7}{4}x + 2$

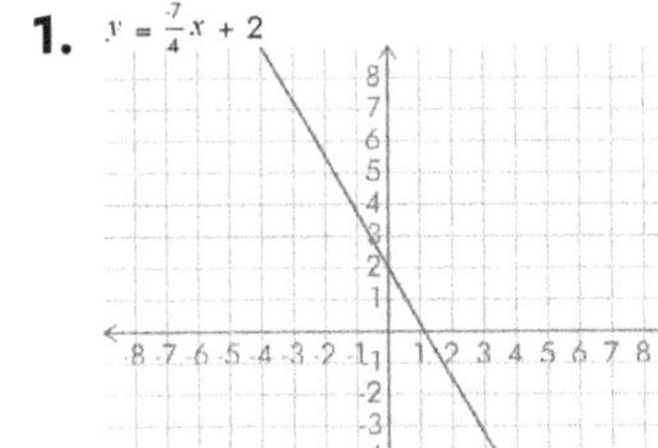

**2.** $y = x + 7$

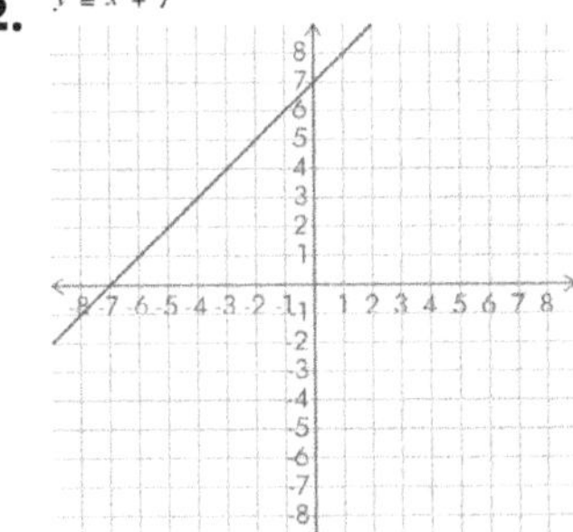

**3.** $y = \frac{-9}{4}x - 2$

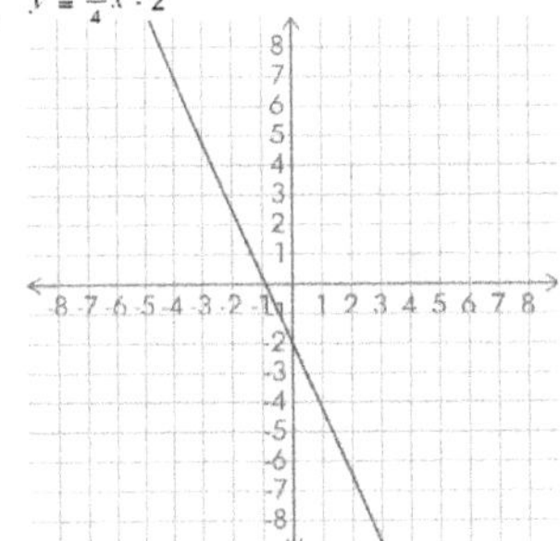

**4.** $y = -2$

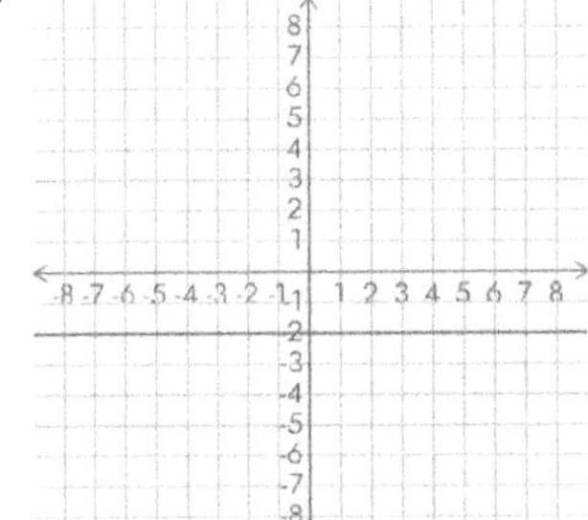

**5.** $y = \frac{1}{4}x - 8$

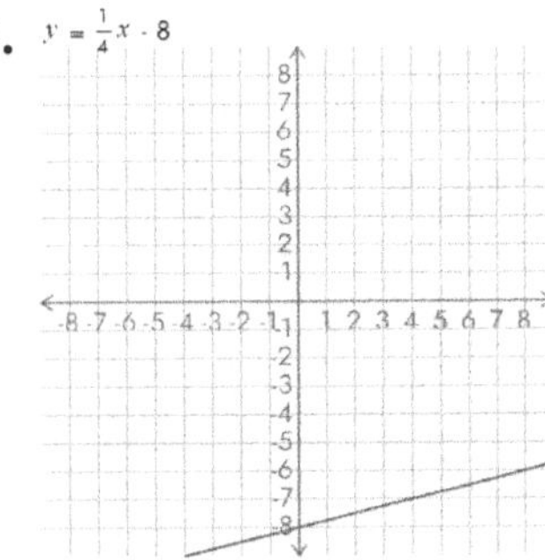

## Page 51: System of Equations

1. x = 8.5, y = -5.0
2. x = 2.4, y = -1.8
3. x = 1.64, y = -1.18
4. x = -0.25, y = 0.75
5. x = 5.57, y = -9.43
6. x = -2.93, y = 3.71
7. x = -6.0, y = 10.0

8. x = 0.55, y = 0.52
9. x = 8.0, y = -11.0
10. x = 0.91, y = 0.66
11. x = -29.0, y = 34.0
12. x = 1.25, y = -0.5
13. x = -0.23, y = 0.62
14. x = 2.7, y = -3.3

15. x = -0.3, y = 1.54
16. x = -4.6, y = 7.0
17. x = 2.23, y = -0.54
18. x = 1.89, y = -5.11
19. x = 8.0, y = -14.0
20. x = 0.29, y = 1.57

## Page 58: Quadratic Equations

1. No real solution
2. (-0.905, 0.905)
3. (1.038, -1.401)
4. (10, -9)
5. (1.636, -0.747)
6. (-5, -6)

7. (2.333, -1)
8. (-1, 1)
9. (1, -0.333)
10. (7, -3)
11. (1.806, -0.949)
12. (-2.4, 1)

13. (-4, 4)
14. No real solution
15. (-5.5, 5.5)
16. (-5, -6)
17. (-1.063, 1.881)
18. (-3, 3)